GLIMPSES OF MY LIFE

Glimpses of My Life

A Photographic Journey

by David Rockefeller

Peter J. Johnson & Fraser P. Seitel, Editors
Designed by Marianna S. Schaffer
Separations in four-color process by Frances Beebe
Printed by Polyprint Design on 100% post-consumer recycled paper

CONTENTS

INTRODUCTION

In early 2003, a few months after the publication of my *Memoirs*, Brian Lindquist, a friend and colleague, suggested that it might be interesting to prepare a book that would utilize my collection of photographs. I had begun taking photographs soon after my parents gave me a Brownie camera in the mid 1920s, and I have been at it ever since - albeit with progressively better equipment! I had snapped thousands of pictures of family, friends and acquaintances all over the world during my frequent business trips and vacations and also had hundreds more taken of me by others. It seemed possible that we might be able to devise an interesting photo-essay book using the best of these pictures as the raw material. I also consulted with two other colleagues, Fraser P. Seitel and Peter J. Johnson, who had worked closely with me in the preparation of *Memoirs* and on many other projects over the years. They thought the idea merited further exploration.

Alas, this plan proved to be unworkable. We discovered some serious technical problems. Many of the older photographs, the ones I had taken in the 1920s and 1930s and during my World War II service in North Africa and Europe, had been damaged by time and neglect. There were also some aesthetic issues, as many of the pictures were formal group shots of me standing around with other men in business suits. While often documenting important meetings, these photos were intrinsically uninteresting. But, the biggest obstacle, we decided, was the difficulty of writing an interesting narrative that could knit this eclectic collection together in a compelling way. We decided to go back to the drawing board.

Fortunately, we found a viable alternative. During our initial photo review, we had set aside a number of good shots of historical figures, some of which I had taken myself, including one of Adolph Hitler strutting along Munich's Ludwigstrasse in late 1937. It occurred to us, more or less simultaneously, that we might be able to produce a book that focused on interesting and influential individuals whom I had met at one time or another over the past ninety years. We would write about each of them and use photographs from my personal collection and from other repositories, such as the Rockefeller Archive Center and the JPMorgan Chase Collection. We decided to try that approach, and this book is the result.

How did we select the individuals for inclusion? I have been fortunate during my life to have met, and in many cases gotten to know rather well, men and women who have played critical roles on the world stage. This was particularly true of the years when I was a senior executive with The Chase Manhattan Bank (now JPMorgan Chase & Company). I traveled extensively from the late 1940s until the early 1980s to more than 70 countries to build the bank's international business. And so, for this volume, we decided somewhat arbitrarily to include only individuals from the Middle East and Sub-Saharan Africa. In addition, my work, as well as my interest in various areas of public policy and international affairs, also brought me into close contact with a number of American presidents. I often saw a side of these men that I thought might be of interest to others and decided to include them in this volume as well. Finally, because I was born in New York City and have spent my entire life here, and because I have cared deeply about its well being, I decided to include a number of New York mayors and a few others with whom I have worked during the course of my career.

In addition to Brian Lindquist, Fraser P. Seitel and Peter J. Johnson, with whom I have spent many pleasant hours working on this book, I want to acknowledge with gratitude the essential contributions of a number of other people. Marianna S. Schaffer, who ably handles a portion of my philanthropy, has many other talents as well. She took full responsibility for the exquisite design of this book and oversaw its production as well. Without her, the elegance and superior technical quality of this book would not have been possible. Michele Hiltzik of the Rockefeller Archive Center, Christine Roussel of the Rockefeller Center Archives, and Jean Elliott, Nancy Palley and Shelly Diamond of the JPMorgan Chase & Company Archives worked heroically to find good photographs to supplement those from my own collection. Frances Beebe did much more than print the book; she solved innumerable technical problems with great ability and enormous good humor. I thank all of them for their talent and perseverance.

Again, this volume includes only a handful of the many interesting and influential people I have met over the course of 90+ years. I look forward to considering a possible second volume to include other fascinating friends and acquaintances, as I continue to enjoy this wonderful and fortunate life.

David Rockefeller
December 2009

In northern Syria during World War II, 1944.

On the Pocantico estate in the mid 1930s.

I took this photograph during my trip to Egypt with my parents in the Spring of 1929.

A photograph I took of Hitler on the Ludwigstrasse, December, 1937.

Dedicated to
My Family and Friends

AMERICAN PRESIDENTS

MIDDLE EAST LEADERS

AFRICAN LEADERS

NEW YORK CITY MAYORS

I have been fortunate over my life to have met eleven sitting presidents of the United States, commencing with a brief encounter with Calvin Coolidge. I regret that I never met Herbert Hoover or FDR or Harry Truman, and I look forward to the day that I meet Barack Obama. As to the eleven presidents I have met, I present brief accounts of my experiences with each. The one I admired most was Dwight Eisenhower. The one whose company I enjoyed the most was John Kennedy. The one I found most difficult to relate to was Richard Nixon. In the late 1970s, largely because of the Trilateral Commission (Jimmy Carter and twenty or so of his cabinet and sub-cabinet appointments were members), there were a number of magazine articles contending that "David Rockefeller is running the U.S. government." Fortunately, that was never the case.

Calvin Coolidge and his wife, Grace, on the campaign trail, 1925.

CALVIN COOLDIGE • 1923-1929

The first American president I met was Calvin Coolidge, although only to shake his hand.

I was 10-years old, and my mother took my brother Winthrop and me to Washington during one of our school vacations. One of Mother's brothers, Congressman Richard Aldrich, arranged our visit to the White House. Uncle Richard was the only one of Mother's siblings to follow in the footsteps of his father, Nelson Aldrich, a congressman and senator from Rhode Island for almost four decades. As Republican majority leader in the senate during the 1890s and most of the first decade of the twentieth century, Grandfather Aldrich controlled American monetary and trade policy with an iron hand and was considered to be one of the most powerful politicians in the country.

Uncle Richard never came close to wielding power in the manner of his father, but he did serve five terms in the House of Representatives (1923-33). He was quite a genial fellow and he and Mother were quite fond of one another. At her request, Uncle Richard arranged for us to be included in one of the afternoon receptions held by President Coolidge and his wife. We waited patiently in line and then solemnly grasped the president's hand. He smiled and said hello and chatted briefly with Mother. That was it, but the grandeur of the White House left a lasting impression on me.

Mother, Win and I stayed at the Dodge Hotel in Washington, a YWCA hotel. Mother was an ardent supporter of the "Y" and its mission of providing young, single working women with a safe and wholesome place to live. She even sent Winthrop and me down to the laundry to help sort sheets and towels to give us a better sense of how the hotel operated.

Then it was on to the White House to shake hands with President Coolidge.

General Eisenhower's inauguration as Columbia University's president, October 1, 1948.

DWIGHT D. EISENHOWER • 1953-1961

Everyone who served in North Africa or Europe during the Second World War considered General Eisenhower, "Ike" as he was called, to be his or her commanding officer. I actually saw him on a couple of occasions. As an intelligence officer - a lowly second lieutenant - my unit was attached to Eisenhower's Allied Force Headquarters in Algiers when I joined it in September of 1943. While the fighting war had moved on to Italy by that time, the General still commanded all Allied military and naval forces in the Mediterranean. I glimpsed him striding through the halls, cigarette in hand, or surrounded by aides leaving for an inspection tour or meeting. He seemed friendly, especially when he flashed his famous smile, but remote and unapproachable.

In 1948, Eisenhower became president of Columbia University and a trustee of the Carnegie Endowment for International Peace, which I had recently joined. I talked with him at our monthly board meetings, and he invited me to become a Columbia trustee. I had to decline because of my growing responsibilities at Chase and with not-for-profit institutions.

During that same period in the late 1940s, I did convince the General to work with me on a project. As the chairman of Morningside Heights, Inc., an organization working to develop affordable housing on the Upper West Side of Manhattan, I invited Eisenhower and the heads of the other major institutions - Riverside Church, Union Seminary and others - to join the board and to attend, personally, our monthly meetings. Ike agreed and never missed a meeting during the two years he served at Columbia.

I never found Eisenhower especially comfortable with me or other private sector executives during the few times I met him privately. It was as if he felt "insecure" around successful business people. This always struck me as odd, because I knew few in business who could approach Eisenhower in terms of courage, responsibility and leadership. I greatly respected his vision of the world, his intelligence and his strong unwavering principles.

Indeed, Eisenhower was the best American president of my lifetime.

President Kennedy outlines his position on tax reform, Washington, April 23, 1963.

JOHN F. KENNEDY • 1961 -1963

In January of 1938, halfway through my year of graduate study at the London School of Economics, Ambassador Joseph P. Kennedy invited me to attend the debut of his daughter, Kathleen, at the Embassy Residence. It was a glittering affair. Most of Britain's aristocracy was present along with many political and business leaders. Young Jack Kennedy, then a senior at Harvard, came over for the party. Wearing white tie and tails, it was there that I first shook his hand.

After the War, when he became a senator, we saw each other many times. Jack was always gracious and polished. While he and I differed in our views on many domestic issues, Jack's views on foreign affairs - particularly the threat posed by the Soviet Union - were similar to mine.

In 1958, Jack joined me as a member of the Harvard Board of Overseers. It was a significant honor for him and one of the few affiliations he maintained after his election to the presidency. He even invited the Overseers to meet at the White House and then entertained us at dinner.

Some time later, at another White House dinner, Jack and I chatted about our views on a tax cut to stimulate the sputtering U.S. economy. He asked me to follow up in writing with my thoughts, which I did. The president responded to my letter with one of his own. Henry Luce, the owner of Time-Life (one of the precursors of today's Time Warner) heard about this exchange and asked if he could publish our letters side-by-side in *Life* magazine.

It is a tragedy that Jack's tenure as president was cut short. His death radically altered the trajectory of American history. He was an intelligent, charming and able man - a real leader.

President Johnson announces the creation of the International Executive Service Corps in the White House Rose Garden, May 25, 1967.

LYNDON B. JOHNSON • 1963-1969

I first met Lyndon Johnson at the annual Gridiron Dinner in Washington in the mid 1950s. Johnson had become senate majority leader only a year or so earlier, but he was already one of the most powerful men in the capitol and clearly had his eye on the White House.

Johnson tended to measure you by your potential usefulness to him and valued loyalty very highly. He was very warm and charming, but exceptionally thin-skinned. In the mid 1960s I gave a speech in Chicago criticizing Johnson's "guns and butter" policy as dangerously inflationary because he was simultaneously enacting his Great Society program and escalating the Vietnam War without, at least in my view, any thought to the fiscal and budgetary consequences. I was certainly not alone in stating my misgivings publicly, but a few months later as I was leaving a meeting in the White House with a number of other people, he suddenly shouted across the room, "How could you ever make a speech like that?"

Despite those occasional moments of tension, Johnson and I got along well together. He was one of the few presidents I have known who really took Latin America seriously and backed policies that would make a difference in both economic development and positive political change. He eagerly sought the cooperation of the private sector in the United States and listened to our views.

Henry Kissinger and I listen to President Nixon speak about U.S.-Latin American Relations at the White House, November 6, 1969.

RICHARD M. NIXON • 1969 -1974

I have often met famous people and celebrities who are not at all the way they have been characterized in the popular press. Richard Nixon was the exception. As advertised, he was a strange man - a rather cold person.

Nixon asked me twice, through intermediaries, to join his Administration. In neither instance, did he ask me himself. Rather, the first time in 1968, he relayed word though Nelson that he wanted me to be his first secretary of the treasury. I told Nelson that since I was just becoming chairman of Chase, I would have to decline. A few days later, I paid a courtesy call on Nixon and, although we spoke for almost two hours, the president-elect never brought up the treasury secretary post.

In 1974, I was in Kuwait and got a telephone call from Al Haig, Nixon's chief of staff. Al said that George Schultz planned to step down as treasury secretary and that the president would like me to replace him. When I returned from my trip, I sat with Haig to discuss the position. Upon reflection, I felt that the difficult economic measures necessary might be difficult for a person named "Rockefeller" to impose. Once again, I respectfully declined the president's invitation. I suspect Nixon, who disliked being turned down, was none too pleased with my decisions.

Years later after his ignominious White House departure, Nixon lived next door to me in Manhattan. When he first moved in, I invited him over for lunch. It took two years for him to return the invitation. On his last day in the house, before moving to New Jersey, he invited Henry Kissinger and me to lunch.

With Gerald Ford and others at the White House, October 18, 1975.

My brother Nelson and President Gerald Ford at the swearing in of Edward Levi as Attorney General, February 7, 1975.

Gerald R. Ford • 1974-1977

Gerald Ford faced as difficult a set of challenges as any American president, at least until Barack Obama was inaugurated in January of 2009. As the "unelected" successor to the disgraced Richard Nixon, Ford had to ensure the continuity and legitimacy of the American constitutional system and begin to heal the wounds inflicted by the Watergate Crisis at the same time that he had to manage all of the tasks of the chief executive - including the collapse of the South Vietnamese government and the painful defeat of American arms in Indochina. Ford handled this unprecedented political transition with grace, humor and great personal courage.

Ford had always been respectful of Nelson and me, although I felt he, like Richard Nixon, was also somewhat envious of us. Ford's decision in 1975 to drop Nelson as his vice presidential running mate devastated my brother. Years later at a dinner in New York, Ford told me the decision was a mistake and probably lost him the election to Jimmy Carter.

Although I felt Ford looked up to me as a "captain of industry," I may have been wrong. During the City's "Fiscal Crisis" in the fall of 1975, Walt Wriston of Citibank, Pat Patterson of J. P. Morgan and I met with the president, Treasury Secretary William Simon and Federal Reserve Chairman Arthur Burns in the Oval Office in an effort to convince them that a federal guarantee of loans was essential to ending the crisis. Neither Ford nor Bill Simon were receptive to this idea. In fact, a few days later the president vowed to veto any New York City "bailout" bill. This inspired the legendary *New York Daily News* headline, "FORD TO CITY: DROP DEAD." So much for the persuasiveness of "captains of industry."

Greeting President Carter at the White House before a strained meeting on U.S. foreign policy, April 19, 1979.

JIMMY CARTER • 1977-1981

My relationship with President Carter has been a curious and complicated one. Soon after Carter was inaugurated Georgia's governor in 1971, he called and asked if I would be willing to organize a lunch for him in New York with the financial community. I agreed. After lunch, one of his aides took me aside and said, "Mr. Rockefeller, Governor Carter some day wants to be president."

When we organized the Trilateral Commission two years later, we included Governor Carter because he provided both regional and partisan balance as a Southern Democrat with good international credentials. Carter came to every meeting during his three-year term and learned a lot. He also made connections that would serve him well in the future. The surprise winner of the 1976 presidential election, he filled his cabinet with Trilateral members, including Vice President Walter Mondale, Secretary of State Cyrus Vance, National Security Advisor Zbig Brzezinski, Secretary of Treasury Mike Blumenthal, and Secretary of Defense Harold Brown. This was the source of the claims made by conspiracy theorists and even some popular magazines that "David Rockefeller is running the U.S. government."

In mid 1979, Carter first asked me to become secretary of treasury and then chairman of the Federal Reserve. In the first case, I didn't think a Rockefeller presiding over an economic crisis would be a good idea. In the latter, I suggested Paul Volcker would be a better choice. Thankfully, the president followed my advice.

That was not the case with the Shah of Iran. I felt the Carter Administration had made a significant error in abandoning our long time ally in early 1979 when a popular revolution, fueled by Islamic fundamentalism, forced his abdication. After the Shah fled Iran and was asked to leave Morocco, I joined with Henry Kissinger and others in the effort to find a permanent refuge for him and his family. I have written about the Shah elsewhere in this volume. I still believe the Carter Administration's treatment of the Shah was disgraceful.

It was almost twenty years before President Carter and I met again, as members of the official American delegation that participated in the ceremonies marking the final handover of the Panama Canal in 1999. He and I spent a pleasant few hours talking about many things on the flight down, but the subject of Iran never came up.

Although Jimmy Carter made a number of serious mistakes during his time in office, I think he is a fine man who has been a remarkable emissary for the United States in the years after his presidency.

My brother, Laurance, and I talk with President Reagan at Kykuit just before the reopening of the Statue of Liberty, July 3, 1986.

RONALD REAGAN • 1981 -1989

Although my wife, Peggy, and I had probably seen Reagan in one or two movies, I did not meet him until the summer of 1976 at Bohemian Grove. He was most congenial and an excellent raconteur.

After his election, President Reagan appointed my friend Bill Hewitt, the CEO of John Deere & Co., ambassador to Jamaica. The president asked if I would organize a business committee to support Jamaica's newly elected president, Edward Seaga, which I agreed to do. The president also supported my efforts to stimulate private sector housing construction and accepted my invitation to speak to a large and enthusiastic audience in New York.

In 1986, President and Mrs. Reagan accepted my family's invitation to stay at Kykuit during the Statue of Liberty's rededication. While he and Mrs. Reagan were perfectly polite, both seemed rather distant and "on guard" throughout their stay. Nor did the president engage in the kind of "small talk" for which he was well known.

President Reagan played a quiet, but important role in creating the National Museum of the American Indian as well. Presidential action was required to free up the federally owned Customs House on Bowling Green in Lower Manhattan. Museum advocates had tried to interest federal officials in the idea, but to no avail. We realized our only recourse was the president himself. By coincidence, our old friends Archie and Lucky Roosevelt had invited us to a small private dinner in their Washington home with President and Mrs. Reagan. I used the occasion to explain the situation and asked for his help. He said he would consider it, and the very next day we were informed that the president had authorized the General Services Administration to look into the matter. Although a different solution was eventually found, this was an essential step in building the National Museum of the American Indian, which opened on the Mall in Washington in 2004, but continues to operate a significant facility at the New York Custom House.

I was impressed, not only because of Reagan's decisiveness, but also that he was willing to do the right thing.

A friendly conversation with President Bush just before he left office in early 1992.

George H.W. Bush • 1989-1993

I met George Bush in the late 1960s as he was beginning his rise through the ranks of the Republican Party. He was a young, moderate Texas congressman (one of the first Republicans elected in Texas since the end of Reconstruction) and a successful businessman. I knew his father, Senator Prescott Bush of Connecticut, and my brothers and I had invested in the younger Bush's company, Zapata Offshore, which did oil exploration in the Gulf of Mexico. I thought George was destined for great things.

My estimate of his future prospects was quickly confirmed. During the first half of the 1970s, he served as ambassador to the United Nations, chairman of the Republican National Committee, the first ambassador to the People's Republic of China, and director of the Central Intelligence Agency. He performed superbly in each of these difficult assignments.

When he returned to private life in 1977, I immediately invited George to join the Trilateral Commission. He accepted and participated in our conferences. I enthusiastically backed George for the 1980 Republican presidential nomination, which Ronald Reagan won, and again in 1988, when he won the election. In my view, George represented the best traditions of the Republican Party. He was a fiscal conservative and a moderate on social issues. Most importantly, he was a solid internationalist in foreign policy. He managed the end of the Cold War and the collapse of the Soviet Union with prudence and ability and he helped to reorient American policy in this hemisphere through the Caribbean Basin Initiative and the negotiation of the North American Free Trade Agreement. His commitment to a balanced federal budget, especially his willingness to raise taxes, was an act of great political courage, although it doomed him with the increasingly powerful right wing of his own party.

George and I are both left-handed and share the same June 12th birthday. For years we exchanged birthday telegrams to commemorate the day. In my view, George Bush was one of the most competent and effective presidents of my lifetime.

President Clinton and First Lady Hillary Clinton present me with the Presidential Medal of Freedom at the White House, January 15, 1998.

WILLIAM J. CLINTON • 1993-2001

I first met Bill Clinton when he was governor of Arkansas in the 1980s. I was attending a meeting at my late brother Win's ranch on Petit Jean Mountain near Little Rock, where the governor was slated to deliver a speech. He arrived hours late, a disturbing habit he would repeat during his years on the national stage. He hurried in, apologizing profusely, and delivered a compelling address on the importance of agriculture to the future of the world. He spoke for almost an hour without notes, demonstrating a sure grasp of a complex subject, and was totally convincing. I, along with the rest of the audience, was dazzled.

Five years later in 1991, I met Clinton again, this time at a Bilderberg meeting. Clinton was considering a run for the presidency, and Vernon Jordan, one of the Democratic Party's power brokers, brought him to Bilderberg for some international exposure and to introduce him to other opinion leaders. I played a round of golf with the two of them and found Clinton to be charming and well informed about world affairs.

Despite his obvious talents, I was surprised when Clinton defeated President Bush so easily in the 1992 election. However, I have come to recognize that Clinton was probably one of the most skillful politicians of my lifetime. His most impressive initiatives involved crafting domestic and foreign policy measures that addressed the fundamentally transformed world that followed the collapse of the Soviet Union. Those policies were certainly not perfect in all respects, but Clinton worked on them diligently. I think he deserves particular credit for his tireless work to create a comprehensive solution to the Israeli-Palestinian dispute. He also helped create the World Trade Organization, fought tenaciously for the passage of the North American Free Trade Agreement and also put into place the diplomatic structure to create the Free Trade Area of the Americas.

I was deeply honored to have President Clinton present me with the Presidential Medal of Freedom at a ceremony in the East Room of the White House on January 15, 1998. Sadly, well-known and indefensible personal actions tarnished Bill Clinton's otherwise admirable presidency.

Introducing President Bush at the Council of the Americas conference in Washington, May 7, 2001.

GEORGE W. BUSH • 2001-2009

In December of 2006, my daughter Neva and I attended a White House dinner in honor of Kofi Annan, who was retiring as secretary-general of the United Nations. I had met President Bush only briefly on a few occasions, so I was pleased to be seated at his table. I found him cordial, personable and quite likable. He was a first-rate host and a warm and friendly individual.

On the other hand, as a president of the United States, George W. Bush was a disappointment. Not a student of history nor widely traveled before his election, he adhered to a narrow, conservative ideology throughout most of his tenure. Bush governed as a partisan and ended up alienating a significant portion of the American people. In fairness, his tough policies on homeland security kept the country safe from more terrorist attacks after the shock of 9/11. This significant accomplishment could not overcome his mishandling of the Iraq war, the poor response to the devastation of Hurricane Katrina, and during his final years in office, the worst financial crisis since the Great Depression.

George Bush's presidency ended on a dismal note. I suspect history will not assess him with kindness.

Looking back, it seems as if I have had a connection with the Middle East for most of my life. I first visited Egypt and the Holy Land as a thirteen-year old on a trip with my parents in the Spring of 1929. I was stationed in Algiers during World War II and traveled throughout North Africa and as far as Istanbul for my work as an intelligence officer.

After the war, as an officer of the Chase Bank, I visited the Middle East on a regular basis, at one point two or three times a year. Those trips brought me into close contact with many Israeli and Arab leaders, a few of whom, most notably Egyptian President Anwar Sadat, became good friends. In the process of doing the bank's business, I also learned a great deal about the intractable and intertwined political and economic issues of Palestine and petroleum, which have fragmented the region and continue to frustrate and endanger the rest of the world.

Middle East Leaders

Yasser Arafat, Palestine

Menachem Begin, Israel

Moshe Dayan, Israel

Abdel Azis al Ghani, Yemen

Saddam Hussein, Iraq

Sheik Isa bin Salman al Khalifa, Bahrain

Teddy Kollek, Israel

Golda Meir, Israel

Molay Hassan ben Mohammad, Morocco

Sheik Zayed al Nahyan, Abu Dhabi

Gamal Abdel Nasser, Egypt

Mohammad Reza Pahlavi, Iran

Yitzhak Rabin, Israel

Anwar al Sadat, Egypt

Qaboos bin Said al Said, Oman

Faisal Ibn Abdul al Saud, Saudi Arabia

Ariel Sharon, Israel

Hussein bin Talal, Jordan

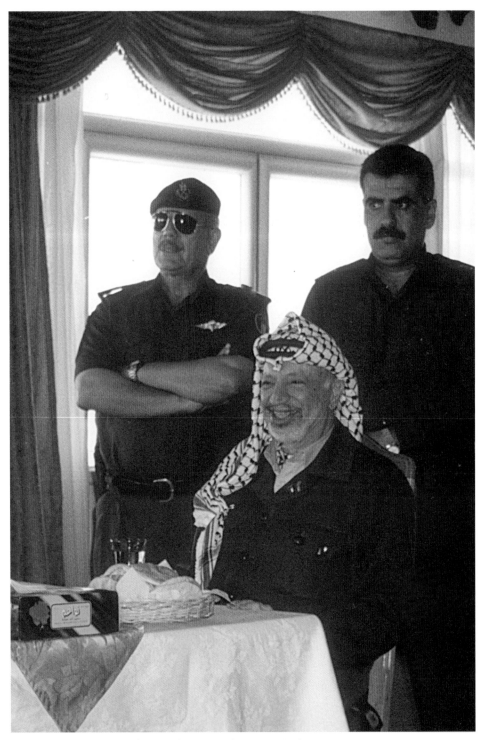

Arafat at a meeting with members of the Council on Foreign Relations, Gaza, October 25, 1999.

Yasser Arafat
President of the Palestinian Authority • 1996-2004

From the late 1960s until the first years of the 21st century, Yasser Arafat (the nom de guerre of Muhammad Abdal Rauf al Qudwah al Husayni) was one of the most powerful men in the Middle East. He held in his hands, at least at certain moments, the fate of countries like Jordan and Lebanon. By the mid 1970s he became the most effective and implacable adversary the Israelis faced in the region.

Arafat's great power was paradoxical: he did not control vast oil wealth, like the Saudis or Kuwaitis, or govern a strategically important country, like Egypt or Iraq. Instead, he led a stateless and impoverished people, many of them confined to squalid refugee camps in Lebanon, the Gaza Strip and the West Bank. In the end, Arafat's power flowed from his control of the Palestine Liberation Organization (PLO) and his unshakeable commitment to the creation of a Palestinian state. Although the PLO was both a political organization and a paramilitary force, the Israelis considered Arafat to be a terrorist. It was not until the 1980s that they agreed to deal with him in an effort to reach an agreement that would establish a viable Palestinian state, preserve Israel's integrity and independence, and put an end to decades of hostility and warfare.

I met Arafat only once, in 1999, during a trip with my friend Pete Peterson and other members of the Council on Foreign Relations to the Middle East. Arafat joined us for a meal at a restaurant in Gaza City. His Parkinson's disease was clearly evident, but he impressed me as still shrewd and tough, much as I had expected. He was in the midst of yet another round of negotiations with the Israelis, which the Clinton Administration was brokering. Arafat answered our questions candidly. He rejected any further compromises in regard to Jerusalem and denounced the continued expansion of Jewish settlements in the West Bank on territory that would be part of the Palestinian homeland. He held to this position tenaciously over the next few years even in the face of Israeli compromises.

After Arafat's death in 2004, the carefully modulated compromises reached over a period of twenty years collapsed. More radical Islamic fundamentalists in Hamas pushed aside Arafat's PLO in Gaza, and progress on the creation of a viable Palestinian state there, and on the West Bank, literally went up in smoke. No real successor to Arafat has yet emerged among the Palestinians.

Meeting with Begin in Jerusalem shortly before he resigned, February 13, 1981.

MENACHEM BEGIN
Israeli Prime Minister • 1977-1983

I found Menachem Begin the toughest and most inflexible of all the Israeli leaders whom I have met. His personal history went a long way towards explaining his ideological rigidity. Born in Poland, Begin fought against both the Nazis and the Russians before escaping to Palestine in the early 1940s. He lost almost his entire family in the Holocaust. After World War II, he masterminded the bombing of the King David Hotel in Jerusalem, the central British military headquarters - an act he was proud to acknowledge in later years.

When I first met Begin in 1977, soon after he had become prime minister, he told me: "The Jewish people have an unchallengeable, eternal, historic right to the Land of Israel, including the West Bank and Gaza, the inheritance of their forefathers." It was a mantra he repeated endlessly. I found it difficult to argue with a man who claimed God as his principal source of information!

For that reason, I was impressed when Begin invited his archenemy, Anwar Sadat, to visit Jerusalem in 1978 to address the Israeli parliament. It was a magical moment, full of hope for the future. Begin and Sadat, facilitated by President Carter, later signed the Camp David Accords - marking what many of us thought at the time was the first step on the path to peace in the Middle East. We may have been right at the time, but sadly, thirty years later we are no closer to real peace now than we were then.

Ruth and Moshe Dayan in Tel Aviv, January 31, 1980.

MOSHE DAYAN

Israeli Minister of Defense • 1967-74 and Foreign Minister • 1977-80

Israel's decisive triumph over the numerically superior forces of Egypt, Syria and Jordan in the 1967 Six Day War introduced the world to Moshe Dayan, the grand strategist of victory. With his bald head and raffish black eye patch, he looked a great deal like the American actor Yul Brynner. He was also a political survivor. Having led Israel to victory in 1967, he also had to accept much of the blame for her less impressive performance after Sadat's pre-emptive attack in the 1973 Yom Kippur War. He fell from power, but returned in 1977 as Menachem Begin's foreign minister.

When I visited the legendary general and his wife at their Tel Aviv home in 1977, he proudly showed me around his garden, filled with the Greek, Roman and Jewish antiquities he had collected over the years. Dayan was open-minded, easy to speak with and aware of the subtleties of politics not only in the Arab world, but also within the American Jewish community.

Preparing for the qat party with Prime Minister Abd Al Ghani, S'ana, Yemen, February, 1978.

ABDEL AZIS AL GHANI

Prime Minister of the Yemen Arab Republic • 1975-1980 and 1983-1990

Abdel Ghani, who studied political science at Colorado College, served as the prime minister of the Yemen Arab Republic twice, from 1975 to 1980 and from 1983 to1990.

I visited Yemen for the first and only time in 1977 to ask if Chase might establish a broader relationship with his government. Upon arrival, our Chase party learned that the prime minister was entertaining friends at his home, some 20 miles from San'a. He left word that we were all invited to his home.

As I recounted in my *Memoirs*, when we arrived at the house, the prime minister greeted us warmly. We found only men in attendance, all sitting along the walls on cushions and listening to Arab music. There were no chairs, tables, or other furniture. Occasionally, two men would get up and dance with each other.

Admittedly, this was a bit unusual. But most peculiar of all was the "refreshment" of choice shared enthusiastically by the guests. Rather than alcohol, which is expressly forbidden in Islamic countries, the guests chewed qat, a rather mild narcotic said to produce hallucinogenic effects.

I quickly was educated on the etiquette of qat. I learned that the leaves of the plant are chewed and then formed into a little ball that one places under the lower lip. If one chews enough of the leaves, over a period of time it will produce an enjoyable experience. I was given a few leaves to chew, which I did, experiencing little taste and no hallucinogenic impact. Frankly, I much preferred good old, straight-up martinis.

The dénouement of my first and only "qat party" came when the prime minister asked me to dance! Even in my considerable experience of seeing the world, this was a first!

Saddam in a characteristic pose, July 6, 1982.

SADDAM HUSSEIN
President of the Republic of Iraq • 1979-2003

I have met a few people in my life who seemed inherently malevolent and treacherous. That is my sense of Saddam Hussein.

My only meeting with him came as a result of Secretary of State Henry Kissinger's request in 1975. Henry and President Ford wanted to include the Iraqis, who did not have diplomatic relations with us, in Middle East peace talks. Henry asked if I might be able to make contact with Saddam through the Iraqi Central Bank. I agreed and arranged a trip to Baghdad.

After some initial difficulties, I was able to arrange a meeting with Saddam that evening. A car drove me to the National Council building on the Tigris River. I was escorted down an endless series of darkened corridors past armed sentries and finally ushered into a small, windowless room where a stern-faced man of average height and sturdy build greeted me coldly. Saddam was not interested in small talk and we got right down to business.

We spoke for more than an hour, through an interpreter. I explained that Kissinger felt it was time to establish a meaningful dialogue. The unsmiling Saddam rejected almost every point I made and attacked the United States for our unwavering support of Israel and despicable treatment of the Palestinians. He also complained about our support of the Shah of Iran and for supplying him with arms to support Iraqi Kurdish rebels. Unless that ended, restoring diplomatic relations would be impossible. This was an issue that really counted and could serve as the basis for discussion between the two countries. I reported this to Henry, and within a few months, shipments of arms and other supplies to the Kurds were ended. This led to a thaw in Iraqi-Iranian relations and, eventually, to the restoration of diplomatic relations between the United States and Iraq.

I believe that engagement with ideological adversaries is superior to refusing to deal with the other side until an impossible number of pre-conditions are met. Sitting down face-to-face with the leaders of a hostile nation can often produce positive results. That was the proximate result of my meeting with the humorless and ruthless Saddam Hussein.

With Sheik Isa in Manama, Bahrain, February, 1978.

SHEIK ISA BIN SALMAN AL KHALIFA
Emir of Bahrain • 1961-1999

Bahrain is truly a marvel. It's just a tiny, flat island in the middle of the Gulf. It had oil and produced pearls, but the oil was running out and synthetics were hurting the pearl business. So Sheik Isa had the vision to convert Bahrain into a financial center. This he did, adding scores of banks and employees, including the Chase. A friend of the United States, he possessed a great knowledge of Middle East politics. He was particularly helpful in providing naval facilities to us at a time when we badly needed them. Sheik Isa gave me a beautiful sword with a gilt scabbard encrusted with real pearls, which today is displayed at Chase's Private Banking headquarters. Over a period of 20 years, I regularly called on him on my annual trips to the Middle East. I once hosted a dinner for Sheik Isa in Tarrytown at our Family's Playhouse, but we did not serve bustards (see p. 58).

Mayor Kollek takes me on one of many walking tours of the Old City of Jerusalem, January 18, 1975.

TEDDY KOLLEK
Mayor of Jerusalem • 1965-1993

I met Teddy Kollek during my first trip to Israel in 1971. I liked him immediately. He had been active in Zionist affairs since his youth and had even negotiated with the infamous Adolph Eichmann for the release of European Jews in the late 1930s. He worked with David Ben-Gurion to create the State of Israel and served as ambassador to the United States in the early 1950s.

Teddy's great love was Jerusalem, and he enjoyed taking visitors through the Old City's cobbled streets and narrow alleyways to the holy sites sacred to Judaism, Islam and Christianity. He took me on four separate tours over the years, and, each time, shared with me a different and compelling aspect of the city's incredible history.

Teddy was the Israeli leader with whom I had the most contact. I was amazed at his energy and the transformation that he had brought to the ancient city. He believed that Jerusalem had to be a place open to people of all faiths and worked tirelessly to achieve that goal.

Sharing a meal with Prime Minister Meir at the Council on Foreign Relations, March 7, 1973.

GOLDA MEIR
Israeli Prime Minister • 1969-1974

I had a lengthy conversation with Prime Minister Meir on my first trip to Israel in 1971. It was actually the second time we had met. In 1960, a representative of the Israeli government approached my wife, Peggy, requesting that we host an evening with Pablo Cassals, the world-renowned cellist, in our New York City home to support scholarships for Israeli music students. Although we rarely made our home available for such purposes, in this special case we agreed. A number of Israeli officials, including then Foreign Minister Golda Meir, attended. The evening was a great success; Cassals played brilliantly and more than $50,000 was raised from the one hundred guests.

My meeting in 1971 with prime minister Meir was not quite as cordial. The Israelis were still miffed about my suggestion to President Nixon in late 1969 that the United States should develop a more "balanced" policy in the Middle East. The Israelis and their many outraged American supporters accused me of being pro-Arab or anti-Israeli, and those were the more moderate criticisms. So, I spent much of the next few months explaining my position to Israeli officials and to the press.

At our meeting in 1971, it was clear the prime minister still considered me to be a suspicious character. She was aloof and quite dogmatic about Israel's policies and dismissed my request to strengthen Chase's operations in Israel. I attributed her lack of enthusiasm mainly to her doctrinaire Socialism. Like her mentor, David Ben-Gurion, and other founders of Israel, Meir believed deeply in Socialist principles and had thwarted efforts to create a more market-oriented economy. While the distortions in the Israeli economy were already apparent - significant and growing inflation - she was uninterested in listening to an American banker talk about alternatives.

She did warmly recall, however, our evening together in Manhattan a decade earlier.

King Hassan at Hudson Pines, May 27, 1982.

Molay Hassan ben Mohammad
King of Morocco • 1961-1999

King Hassan was an unusual Arab leader. Openly pro-Western at a time when most leaders in the region expressed a deep and unremitting hostility for the United States because of our support of Israel, he still had the trust and respect of even the most radical Middle Eastern leaders, Muamar Ghadafi of Libya and Yasser Arafat of the PLO among them.

Hassan was able to walk this tightrope for two reasons. First, Morocco's location on the far northwestern periphery of the Arab world behind the bulwark of the Atlas Mountains sheltered it from the powerful tensions that gripped much of the region. Second, as a hereditary monarch in a rapidly democratizing world, he knew he had more to gain from cooperation with the West than from trusting in the tender mercies of the radical leaders of the Arab world, many of whom - in Egypt, Libya and Iraq - had achieved power by deposing their own kings. In my view, Hassan made a wise choice and one that enabled him to play an important role as mediator and honest broker throughout his reign.

I first met Hassan in the 1960s, soon after he became king. I found him very approachable, knowledgeable and affable. He also spoke impeccable French. Hassan was a consummate host. He invited Peggy and me to his 60th birthday party celebrations, a moveable feast that went on for weeks and moved from place to place in Morocco. In Marrakech, hundreds of guests filled a huge Bedouin tent set up on the palace grounds. Late in the afternoon, we watched a large contingent of Berber horsemen, mounted on beautiful Arabian horses charge across the plain, brandishing swords and ululating in Hassan's honor.

While we were still in Morocco, Peggy told King Hassan, offhandedly, how much she liked the tent. A few months after our return, one of the king's chamberlains called to say a gift would be delivered that day to our Hudson Pines home. A truck soon arrived and a crew of men unloaded a large tent, which they then assembled on our back lawn! As a thank you, we invited King Hassan to a lunch in his honor at the Playhouse. He arrived two hours late, but never called to say he would be delayed nor did he apologize for any inconvenience he may have caused. Such are the prerogatives of royalty.

During a later visit to Morocco, Joseph Reed and I called on the king in Marrakech. After a short audience, Hassan invited us to accompany him on his trip to Rabat. We agreed, thinking we would be flying there in one of the king's jets. Instead, he led us onto a bus, specially fitted with a throne. The king sat on the throne as we drove through the countryside, while the rest of us sat on comfortable benches along the walls, drinking tiny cups of mint tea. Whenever we entered a village, the bus slowed, and Hassan arose from the throne and stood in the well of the bus, waving at his subjects who lined the streets. It was interesting to observe this traditional display of royal authority, but it took forever to reach Rabat!

My introductory meeting with Sheik Zayed at the Abu Dhabi airport, February, 1978.

SHEIK ZAYED AL NAHYAN

Emir of Abu Dhabi • 1966-2004

I met Sheik Zayed, the hereditary ruler of Abu Dhabi, in the mid 1970s as part of my effort to expand Chase's operations in the Middle East. He was a very impressive man. A Bedouin with a commanding personality, he had also seen a great deal of the world and knew that his small country and the United Arab Emirates had to change so as not to be overwhelmed by the forces of modernity.

At the time, the "city" of Abu Dhabi was not terribly impressive. It was essentially a village of mud-walled huts placed haphazardly along the coastal lowlands. Sheep and goats wandered everywhere along the unpaved streets. A large fort, British-built, dominated the scene. In the absence of a more suitable structure, the fort served as the seat of Abu Dhabi's essentially nomadic government. But, Abu Dhabi and the other members of the newly created United Arab Emirates had huge reserves of petroleum and natural gas. Western oil companies had just started to develop those resources at the time I made that visit.

Sultan Zayed and his compatriots eagerly embraced the idea of a stronger relationship with Chase and other western banks. They followed that strategy for the next thirty years and have become one of the centers of world finance.

Today, of course, Abu Dhabi and Dubai have transformed themselves into glistening, modern cities complete with luxury condominiums, golf courses, five star hotels, indoor ski slopes and the world's largest shopping mall. It is an almost unprecedented change in terms of the scale, the brief time during which it has occurred and the departure from the previous norms of the Arab world. Whether this is appropriate or sustainable, only time will tell.

On a subsequent trip, Sheik Zayed had just returned from falcon hunting in Pakistan. I asked what he had hunted and he told me, bustards, which I learned were large game birds that follow the seasons from Russia to Africa. He said they were delicious and asked me where I was headed next. I said I would go to Bahrain to see Sheik Isa. His eyes glowed with delight. "That is fine, because Sheik Isa has a wonderful cook, who knows how to prepare bustards." So he packed them for us and sent us on our way. When we arrived in Bahrain, Sheik Isa dispatched the birds to his chef, and the following day we had them at a picnic lunch on a hillside overlooking San'a, the capital of South Yemen. Alas, they were rather tough.

Gamal Nasser and King Hussein of Jordan in Eqypt, June, 1967.

GAMAL ABDEL NASSER
President of the Arab Republic of Egypt • 1958-1970

Nasser was one of the Army officers who overthrew King Farouk in 1952 and established the Egyptian republic. In 1956, Nasser's actions during the Suez Crisis made him a hero in the Middle East. He became the prophet of a new Arab nation stretching from Morocco to the Indian Ocean and vowed to create an Egypt free from capitalist influences. He signed a treaty of friendship with the Soviet Union that provided him with the financing to build the Aswan Dam, believed by many to be the key to Egyptian economic development. Nasser's opposition to Israel and anti-Western rhetoric made him the most popular and influential leader in the Arab world.

Eugene Black, former president of the World Bank, believed Nasser was less hostile to the West than his rhetoric suggested. Gene arranged for me to see Nasser in December of 1965. We met in his Cairo office, filled with photos of world leaders, few of them European and none from the United States. I found Nasser self-confident, brash and convinced the Arabs would drive the Israelis "into the sea" within a short time. Despite his posturing and obvious displeasure with U.S. policy, I also discovered a surprising flexibility on some issues and an eagerness to maintain a dialogue with me.

Four years later, in the wake of his humiliating defeat by Israel in the 1967 War, Nasser summoned me to an urgent meeting in Cairo. Egypt had broken off diplomatic relations with the United States, and I first cleared the trip with Henry Kissinger, Nixon's national security advisor. We met at Nasser's home in early October of 1969. He was a changed man, ravaged by the diabetes that would kill him within a year and trapped by his growing political and military weakness. Nasser spoke candidly of the radicalism sweeping the Middle East that might destabilize the region unless the Arab-Israeli conflict was quickly ended. When I told him I would be meeting with President Nixon when I returned home, he urged me to pass on his concerns. I noticed Nasser had removed his entire photo collection with the exception of an inscribed picture from Lyndon Johnson.

I think Nasser realized that Egypt was an economic and financial disaster. If he had lived longer, he might have followed the path pursued by his successor, Anwar Sadat.

Discussing the impact of the OPEC Oil Embargo with the Shah in the Royal Palace in Tehran, November, 1974.

MOHAMMAD REZA PAHLAVI
Shahanshah and Aryamehr of Iran • 1941-1979

Mohammad Reza Pahlvai's government had been a correspondent banking client of the Chase for many years. It was in that context that I had limited contact with the Shah of Iran, who referred to me as "Mr. Rockefeller," while I always addressed him as "Your Imperial Highness."

In the 1970s, I sought a direct Chase presence in Iran and met the Shah in St. Moritz, where he was skiing. This was the time of the first Oil Shock and the Shah clearly wanted to cash in on the rapidly increasing price of petroleum. I listened for over two hours to his outsized expectations for an Imperial Iran and was struck by how little the Shah seemed concerned about the global dislocations caused by the high price of oil. He focused solely on Iran's new role in the world. He did, however, allow the bank to expand, and our business grew materially.

Results were not as beneficial for Iranians. Despite its new wealth, the Shah could not solve the nation's underlying problems. In January 1979, the Shah fled. It was clear to me that he deserved asylum in the United States. But President Carter refused, and our longtime ally became, in Henry Kissinger's words, like the "Flying Dutchman," forever cast adrift in the world with no place to call home. Henry and I were incensed that the U.S. had turned its back on an ally. Acting privately and on our own, we finally found a permanent refuge for him and his family in Cuernavaca, Mexico.

And that's where I thought the matter would end, until I was notified in October of 1979 that the Shah's lymphoma had worsened and he would need to come to New York for treatment. I appealed to President Carter, who allowed the Shah temporary entry on humanitarian grounds. I visited him for the last time and found a sick, gaunt and beaten man. He shook my hand and thanked me for my help over his long ordeal.

In the wake of the Shah's admission to the U.S. and the subsequent hostage crisis, the press and many others denounced Henry and me for "forcing" President Carter to give the Shah sanctuary. I continue to believe Henry and I had done the right thing. It was a sad chapter in the history of our country, and, as it turned out, an unforgettable episode in my own life.

A pleasant conversation with Prime Minister Rabin in Jerusalem, January 18, 1975.

YITZHAK RABIN
Israeli Prime Minister • 1992-1995

Yitzhak Rabin commanded the Israeli army in the 1967 Six Day War, a decisive victory over the combined forces of Egypt, Syria, Jordan and Iraq. He emerged from the conflict a hero and made the successful transition to politics - and then the even more difficult evolution into a statesman.

Rabin's quiet persistence in his talks with Yasser Arafat and President Clinton in the early 1990s resulted in real progress towards a "two state solution" to the Israeli-Palestinian stalemate and the so-called "road map" to achieve it. Rabin and Shimon Peres, his political partner in the negotiations, and Yasser Arafat received the Nobel Peace Prize for this effort.

Rabin was one of the more impressive individuals I encountered during the thirty years when I traveled regularly to the Middle East. He was an engaging and sophisticated man who was quite well-educated. He spoke English, but with a strong accent and a pronounced lisp. It was difficult from time to time to understand him clearly. He had a balanced approach to foreign policy, stemming from an instinctive sympathy with the Palestinians and their desire for peace and a secure homeland. He also had a sure grasp of what was politically possible in the cauldron of Israeli domestic politics and the patience to move his people along slowly.

The last time I saw Rabin was at the reception for heads of state at the United Nation's 50th Anniversary in October of 1995. Two weeks later, a right wing extremist assassinated him at a rally in Tel Aviv. It was a great loss for his country and the world.

Greeting my friend Anwar Sadat on a visit to Cairo, March 5, 1977.

ANWAR AL SADAT
President of the Arab Republic of Egypt • 1970-1981

Sadat was a charismatic man with great personal charm and a strong belief in his ability to bring peace to the Middle East. He and I shared a friendship that was rare in my experience with world leaders. It was because I thought our friendship was strong, that I was startled at how quickly it almost ended in 1981.

I first met Sadat in September of 1973. Because Egypt did not have diplomatic relations with the U.S., Henry Kissinger asked me to deliver an important message to the Egyptian President. Henry wanted Sadat to know that lessening tensions with Egypt was one of his highest priorities. I agreed to carry out the assignment and met with Sadat at his home near Alexandria. At the meeting, Sadat surprised me by asking if Chase would be interested in opening an office in Cairo. No foreign bank had been allowed to operate in the country since Nasser's nationalization in the 1950s. I told him we would be interested, but asked how he would feel if Chase opened an office in Tel Aviv. He smiled. "Mr. Rockefeller," he said mysteriously, "it is all a matter of timing." The "mystery" was solved two weeks later. Egypt and her allies launched a surprise attack on Israel. The Yom Kippur War had begun.

Sadat and I developed a close relationship after that and saw each other often. Then, I made a careless mistake. While on a farewell tour of Europe in 1980, an Egyptian banker, claiming to represent Sadat, invited Chase to participate in an Egyptian joint venture bank. After a cursory review, we declined, and I asked an aide to relay the message to the Egyptian banker. And there, the matter ended - or so I thought. I learned later that President Sadat was not used to being "turned down." He was furious with Chase's decision and even more furious that I hadn't called him directly to tell him of the decision. On two subsequent trips to Cairo, and despite a handwritten letter of apology, Sadat refused to see me.

It was more than a year before Sadat finally forgave me. After a speech to the Council on Foreign Relations, Sadat invited me back to the Egyptian mission. We chatted amiably for some time and then parted, friends once again. Not once during our conversation did he mention the issue that had led to our estrangement. Two months later, Sadat was dead, assassinated by Muslim extremists while reviewing a military parade in Cairo commemorating his triumph in the 1973 Arab-Israeli war.

With Sultan Qaboos at a Decatur House Reception in Washington, January 10, 1975.

Qaboos bin Said al Said
Sultan of Oman • 1970-present

Qaboos rose to power in the early 1970s, leading a coup that forced his tyrannical father from the throne. The young sultan's sudden ascent signified to the few people in the United States who studied this part of the world that basic political and economic changes might be in the offing among the small and newly independent states of the Persian Gulf. Oman was a particularly important country. Its significant oil reserves were just being developed in the early 1970s. Even more importantly, the country borders the strategic Straits of Hormuz through which a significant portion of the world's crude oil passes every day. Qaboos let it be known that he wanted to align his country more closely with the United States and that he would welcome American business investment. That was the initial reason for my trip there in 1974.

Qaboos had been educated in India and England, graduated from Sandhurst and served for a time in the British army. He is a handsome man with an erect military bearing, a full beard and dark, piercing eyes. He often wears an elegant turban and beautiful flowing robes with a jewel-studded curved dagger in his belt.

At the time of my arrival, the sultan was trying to suppress an insurrection in the western province of Dhofar, supported by the radical government of South Yemen. He asked us to come to Salalah, his southern capital, to meet him. Rebel sharpshooters and antiaircraft guns were sited in the hills overlooking the city. Our long, low approach over the water to avoid their fire impressed the sultan, and the meeting came off rather well. Over the ensuing years, he and I developed a good relationship.

I called on Sultan Qaboos again in January of 1979. During our meeting, I learned that my brother Nelson had just died of a heart attack. The sultan immediately extended his condolences and offered to send me back to New York in his private plane. It was a wonderful gesture that I have always remembered.

King Faisal al Saud at Islamic Summit Conference, September 1, 1969.

FAISAL IBN ABDUL AL SAUD
King of Saudi Arabia • 1964-1975

King Faisal was the third son of Saudi Arabia's founder, the legendary desert warrior, Ibn Saud. I knew Faisal rather well over an extended period, first meeting him in Riyadh, before he became king, and seeing him for the last time in January 1975, three months before a deranged nephew assassinated him.

Faisal was a dominant and powerful leader. He had an angular nose, dark eyebrows and goatee, and piercing, menacing eyes. There was no question when one was in the room with Faisal as to who was in charge.

Faisal became king in 1964, after a protracted struggle with his elder brother, Saud, who preceded him on the throne. Where Saud was wasteful with the Kingdom's resources, Faisal was a prudent steward of Saudi Arabia's oil wealth. King Faisal modernized the country, established a modern judicial system, invested in infrastructure and universities, including the education of women - even though Faisal strictly observed all dictates of the Muslim religion. He was, by every measure, a most successful monarch and a strong U.S. ally.

I saw Faisal consistently in the 1960s, visiting him on trips for Chase and even hosting a lunch for him at Hudson Pines in 1966. In 1969, after seeing Nasser in Egypt, I visited the king in Riyadh. After the ritual exchange of gifts, Faisal railed against U.S. policy that "favored Israel and U.S. Zionists." He warned that because of that policy, "the U.S. is steadily losing friends and influence in the Middle East." His language was harsh, his tone adamant and those intimidating eyes bored right through me.

Frankly, much of the king's diatribe was bizarre - for example, that "the Israelis are a godless people" and that "the Israelis and Soviets have a secret understanding." It was futile trying to counter his arguments. I told the king I would report to President Nixon everything he had told me, which I did upon my return from the Mid East. After that meeting, Secretary of State William Rogers gave a speech suggesting a more conciliatory posture toward the Arab states. In short order, word leaked to *The New York Times* that I had urged Nixon to adopt a "pro-Arab position" to protect Chase's economic self-interest. Critics besieged the bank with letters, phone calls and ads condemning my "anti-Israel bias," and I eventually had to issue a public statement clarifying my true position.

This unpleasantness aside, my relationship with King Faisal was a fond one. At my last meeting with him in 1975, he presented me with a gilt and diamond sword, which is still displayed at the bank's New York headquarters.

Ariel Sharon near the Temple Mount, Jerusalem, May 31, 1992.

ARIEL SHARON
Israeli Prime Minister • 2001-2005

My only meeting with Ariel Sharon occurred on a visit to Israel in February of 1981. I had visited a number of Arab countries before arriving in Israel and heard the usual complaints about Israeli policy and American support of it. This time, however, they focused on a new topic: the Begin government's policy of aggressively building new settlements and expanding old ones on land captured during the 1967 War. Anwar Sadat, King Hussein of Jordan and others believed these settlements to be a violation of the spirit of the 1980 Camp David Accords, and they feared they could derail a broader peace settlement by giving Yasser Arafat and the extremists in the Palestinian movement a powerful new grievance.

Although I had no reason to doubt Sadat or King Hussein, I thought it best to see these controversial settlements firsthand and make up my own mind. For that reason, my associates called Sharon, the chairman of the Ministerial Committee for Settlements, to arrange a tour of one of the new settlements close to Jerusalem. Sharon offered to conduct the tour personally and assured us the visit would be kept private, as we requested.

I was stunned when I stepped from the car at the settlement and found dozens of reporters and TV cameramen charging at me and shouting the same question, "Mr. Rockefeller, is it true the Chase Bank is loaning the Israeli government two billion dollars for settlement construction?" I told them that was untrue. I was there "purely as an observer to see the settlements firsthand." I complained to Sharon that he had violated our agreement and felt he had entrapped the bank and me. Sharon denied having anything to do with the situation, although we later learned his office had released a detailed itinerary of our tour.

Sharon had a distinguished military career and built his subsequent political career around a hard-line approach to Israel's Arab neighbors and the Palestinians. He was a member of the Likud Party and through an unusual series of events became prime minister in 2001. At that point, with the latest Arab intifada raging, work on the implementation of the Palestinian peace agreement stalled. With tensions rising throughout the Middle East in the wake of September 11th, Sharon changed direction, withdrew Israeli forces from Gaza and offered to negotiate the status of settlements in the West Bank. It was a stunning reversal of Sharon's position, and for a brief period, it looked like the Israelis and Palestinians might reach an accord.

With King Hussein on the tarmac in Amman, Jordan, March, 1967.

Hussein bin Talal
King of the Hashemite Kingdom of Jordan • 1952-1999

Next to Anwar Sadat, perhaps my closest relationship in the Middle East was with King Hussein of Jordan. Like Sadat, Hussein was a man of culture and of strength. Hussein became king at the age of 16, after the assassination of his grandfather and the abdication of his father. King Hussein ruled Jordan for more than four decades of the Arab-Israeli conflict, uniquely balancing the pressures of Arab nationalism with openness to compromise. This willingness to work to resolve the conflict eventually led to a peace treaty with Israel that Hussein negotiated with Israeli Prime Minister Yitzhak Rabin in 1994. So strong were Hussein's ties to Rabin that when Rabin was assassinated a year later, the king delivered a powerful and emotional speech at his funeral in Jerusalem.

During his years on the throne, King Hussein survived numerous assassination attempts, including several occasions when the King personally fought off assailants. He also proved himself a trusted friend of the United States.

I greatly admired King Hussein and always tried to visit him when I traveled to the Middle East. In 1971 on a Chase trip, accompanied by my wife and our daughter Peggy, I stopped briefly in Jordan. Amman was an armed camp, threatened by Yasser Arafat's Mujahadeen forces, which had been forced out of the West Bank after the 1967 War with Israel. The king had taken direct command of his army and established his headquarters outside the city. I left the two Peggys on the plane and was driven alone to see the king for lunch. But when I told him that my wife and daughter had remained on the plane, King Hussein was upset he had not invited them also. He insisted on flying me back to Amman in his helicopter, which he personally piloted, and then boarded the plane to apologize. He even gave daughter Peggy his card and private phone numbers.

In the late 1950s, I watched in amazement as the European colonial empires in Africa, which I thought might last forever, began to crumble. Almost overnight, dozens of new nations emerged, from tiny Gambia to the Congo and Sudan, both more than three times the size of Texas.

I thought the Chase, along with other banks and Western governments, needed to play a central role in the region's economic development. Without outside capital and expertise, I feared that economic growth would stagnate and political instability and social collapse would follow. Despite our best efforts and intentions, this has been the case in all too many of the new states of Sub-Saharan Africa over the past fifty years. I wish it could have been different.

I traveled across the continent a number of times in the 1960s, 1970s and 1980s and met many of the men who had led their nations to independence and continued to rule. They were remarkable individuals - capable, disciplined, politically astute and often charismatic leaders. The most impressive of them all was Nelson Mandela, perhaps the most humane and compassionate man I have ever encountered.

African Leaders

Haile Selassie, Ethiopia

Felix Houphouet-Boigny, Côte d'Ivoire

Sekou Touré, Guinea

Kenneth Kaunda, Zambia

Jomo Kenyatta, Kenya

Omar Bongo, Gabon

Samora Machel, Mozambique

Nelson Mandela, South Africa

Emperor Haile Selassie with my brother, John, at the Rainbow Room in Rockefeller Center, 1962.

HAILE SELASSIE (RAS TAFARI MAKONNEN)

Emperor of Ethiopia • 1930-1974

I met the "Lion of Judah" for the first time in 1959, when my wife, Peggy, and I visited Ethiopia as part of a delegation representing Chase and the Council of Foreign Relations. Among other distinctions, Rastafarians, centered mainly in Jamaica, the United States and Great Britain, revere Selassie as "God incarnate" who would lead the peoples of Africa and the African Diaspora into a golden age of peace and prosperity.

By the time of our visit, Selassie was in his mid 60s and had been emperor for nearly three decades. He was a legendary figure - heir to a dynasty tracing its origins back to King Solomon and the Queen of Sheba. His nation had also been the first victim of Fascist aggression in the 1930s. I remember listening to his eloquent speech before the League of Nations on the radio when he begged for assistance to thwart Mussolini's brutal campaign. Selassie's standing and willingness to fight alongside the Allies led to Ethiopia becoming a charter member of the United Nations, one of only two African nations to be admitted to the new organization.

In 1959, the emperor accorded our group a formal audience in the Royal Palace in Addis Ababa. And that's precisely what it was, "formal." A court chamberlain announced our names, and we walked slowly down the long hall towards the emperor, who sat on a throne elevated well above the floor. We bowed when we reached him and proceeded to make small talk for about 15 minutes. At the conclusion of this brief audience, we filed out of the throne room backwards and bowed again at the door before leaving.

Although the meeting with Selassie was uneventful, I did, on departing, have a memorable brush with one of the emperor's pets. Selassie, as befit the "Lion of Judah," kept several "tame" lions around the palace. One wandered by as we were leaving, and I reached out my hand to pet what appeared to be a docile creature. The lion stopped, peered at me and then let out a low and menacing growl. I quickly headed for the exit.

President Houphouet-Boigny and I touring his hometown, Yamoussoukro, Côte d'Ivoire, March, 1982.

FELIX HOUPHOUET-BOIGNY
President, Republique de Côte d'Ivoire • 1960-1993

Houphouet was educated in French colonial schools and worked as a physician in the Côte d'Ivoire before entering politics in the mid 1940s. First elected to the French National Assembly in 1945, he served in Paris as an overseas deputy closely aligned with the Communist Party for the next sixteen years. Houphouet gained respect from his colleagues, however, by pressing successfully to reform working conditions and to improve public health and schools in all of France's African colonies. Eventually, Houphouet served as a cabinet minister in the 1950s and was even a signatory along with Charles de Gaulle and other notables of the 1959 Constitution of the Fifth Republic.

Houphouet continued to distance himself from his radical origins. In particular, he adopted a moderate position on Ivorian independence from France, one that differed dramatically from the radical nationalist and Marxist alternatives adopted by most of his contemporaries. This approach paid handsome dividends for the Côte d'Ivoire, which enjoyed a stable political environment, strong foreign investment and solid economic growth for the three decades he served as president.

I came to know Houphouet well and visited him several times after Chase established a development bank there in the mid 1960s. The president always treated me warmly; we spoke French and dined together frequently. On one trip, Houphouet arranged for me to be made a chief of his Baoule tribe and presented me with all the robes and symbols of authority.

On a few trips we flew from the capital of Abidjan over hundreds of miles of lush tropical vegetation to the president's boyhood home of Yamoussoukro. There, in the middle of the jungle, we landed at a glistening, modern airport and were transported down a brightly lit, eight-lane highway to a magnificent, ornate palace, protected by a moat and one hundred or so sluggish, but lethal, crocodiles. Close to the palace Houphouet had built the world's largest church, the Roman Catholic Basilica of Our Lady of Peace. It was an amazing sight.

Sekou Touré treated me to one of the most lavish and enthusiastic receptions I have ever received, Conakry, Guinea, 1982.

Sekou Touré and me in Conakry, Guinea, March, 1982.

SEKOU TOURÉ
President of Guinea • 1958-1984

Sekou Touré led his nation to independence from France in 1958, but in an affront to Gallic pride, refused to allow Guinea to become a member of the French Community. As a result, the French left the tiny country in shambles on their way out.

Unfortunately, Sekou Touré made matters worse by choosing a Marxist path to economic development and Lenin as his model for political management. Over the next two decades, he earned the sobriquet, "Father of African Socialism," and by the late 1970s, when I hosted a lunch for him and his entourage (incongruously at the River Club in Manhattan), Guinea was an economic disaster. The West African nation had one of the world's largest reserves of bauxite and other mineral and agricultural resources, but no way of attracting foreign capital to finance their development. It was one of the world's poorest nations.

Sekou Touré knew he had to move in a different direction and signaled that he now understood the importance of the free market. Chase wanted to expand its presence in Africa, and I agreed to visit his country, which I did in 1982 after I had retired, at Bill Butcher's request.

Our party landed in Conakry to find the president, himself, waiting at the airport in a white Cadillac convertible, with a sticker from the Potamkin dealership in New York City on the front grille and a fleet of limousines for the rest of the group. Sekou Touré had declared our visit a national holiday, and thousands of people lined the streets to view our motorcade, as the president drove and I waved from the passenger seat.

Sekou Touré couldn't have been more hospitable, as he personally and proudly escorted us on a tour of his country. The highlight for me was an impromptu speech I gave in French at the Conakry Amphitheatre, where 5,000 Guineans - all dressed in white under the hot sun - welcomed my words with sustained applause.

Sekou Touré was considered one of Africa's most ruthless rulers - and the people around him, among the most corrupt - but on this memorable trip, he distinguished himself as a concerned and intelligent leader and a most thoughtful host. He died only a few years later, on March 27, 1984 at the Cleveland Clinic, of congestive heart failure. Guinea quickly collapsed into the chaos of political instability and civil war from which it has never quite emerged.

The President Kaunda's visit to One Chase Manhattan Plaza, November 16, 1966.

KENNETH KAUNDA
President of Zambia • 1964-1991

President Kaunda, a strong and friendly man, whom I met on a number of occasions, was known to his people as "KK." Like other African leaders involved in the fight for independence, Kaunda spent time in prison. In 1964, after years of struggle, he became the first president of independent Zambia.

In his first years in office, Kaunda concentrated on improving Zambia's educational system, considered one of the worst in the world. Kaunda instituted a policy where all children, irrespective of their parents' ability to pay, were given free exercise books, pens and pencils. In time, education in Zambia improved. And, the University of Zambia was opened in Lusake in 1966, largely as a result of the president's persistence.

As chairman of Chase, I met with President Kaunda a number of times in New York and also visited him in the State House in Lusaka on a couple of occasions, including on a Chase trip after I retired.

Sadly, as things too often happen in Africa, Kaunda's later years in office were marked by strife and discontent. By the mid 1980s, due partly to high commodity prices, misguided domestic policies and the effort to nationalize basic industries, Zambia became one of the world's most indebted nations. When threatened with opposition, Kaunda attempted to impose "one party rule."

Eventually, he was persuaded to introduce a more democratic form of government and left office in 1991 to take up residency, for a time, in Boston.

Jomo Kenyatta with Tom Mboya at the London negotiations that led to Kenya's independence, September 25, 1963.

JOMO KENYATTA
President of Kenya • 1964-1978

Jomo Kenyatta was one of the legendary leaders of the African struggle against European colonialism, and he emerged as the first leader of independent Kenya in the early 1960s. Although Kenyatta was born in very modest circumstances in rural Kenya and trained first as a carpenter, he came from a family of importance within the dominant Kikuyu tribe. He became active in the fight against British colonialism as a young man in the 1920s and by the 1950s had achieved a position of leadership in the movement. The British authorities accused him of complicity in the Mau Mau rebellion and imprisoned him for seven years. Popular demonstrations forced his release in 1960, and he led the Kenyan delegation that secured independence a few years later.

Despite dire predictions of chaos and misrule, Kenyatta proved to be an able leader. He adopted a pro-Western and anti-Communist foreign policy and his government favored market-oriented development and effective land reform. For a period of twenty years, Kenya was one of the success stories in post-Colonial Africa.

I met Kenyatta only once on a trip to Kenya in 1973 to attend the first ever International Monetary Fund meeting in Africa. I called on him at Government House in Nairobi. We had a very pleasant conversation, and we were both astonished to discover that we had studied at the London School of Economics at the same time in the mid 1930s. The president had studied under the famous anthropologist Bronislaw Malinowski and earned a BA degree at the same time that I had taken classes in economics with Friederich von Hayek and Lionel Robbins.

Discussing the bank's plans for expansion with President Bongo, Libreville, Gabon, March, 1982.

Omar Bongo
President, the Republic of Gabon • 1967-2009

Bongo was president of Gabon, a small, oil-rich nation in western Africa, which was one of the charter members of the Organization of Petroleum Exporting Countries (OPEC). A small man - standing just less than 5 feet - he wore platform shoes to appear taller.

Bongo was a career politician, who rose to become the country's vice president under Leon M'ba in 1966. M'ba died the next year, and Bongo succeeded him. Despite his diminutive stature, President Bongo held the position until his death in 2009, earning him the distinction as the world's longest-serving ruler, with the exception of a few monarchs.

President Bongo visited New York a number of times during my Chase chairmanship, but the only time I visited his opulent palace in Libreville was on a trip for the bank after my retirement in 1982. What was most curious was that he had several large TV screens on the walls surrounding the dinner table - all of them on.

While the Chase team was interested in expanding the relationship with Gabon regarding oil financing, the president seemed more eager to discuss the possibility of Chase financing a new luxury apartment for him near the United Nations building in New York. When our group reacted dubiously to the prospect of apartment financing, Bongo seemed to lose interest in the whole conversation and instead turned his attention back to the TV monitors overhead.

Machel at a rally in Maputo celebrating the first anniversary of Mozambique's independence, June 25, 1976.

Samora Machel
President of Mozambique • 1975-1986

When I met Samora Machel in April of 1984, he was a man in desperate straits. Machel had assumed power in his resource-rich East African country in 1975 when the Portuguese abruptly withdrew after more than four centuries of colonial control. Unfortunately, everyone with an education and even a modicum of managerial competence - teachers, government officials, businessmen and farmers - left almost immediately, threatened by Machel's revolutionary background and Marxist ideology. The economy quickly collapsed, insurgencies sprang up (some of them covertly supported by the White South African government), and Machel hung on in the capital of Maputo only because of Soviet financial assistance and a Praetorian guard of Cuban soldiers.

Machel realized this situation could not continue. He understood that imposing even more draconian measures might make matters worse rather than better. He tried a very different course, instead. While in Moscow in early 1984 for the funeral of Soviet leader Yuri Andropov, Machel spoke with Portuguese Prime Minister Mario Soares about his dilemma. Machel felt the only way forward was to attract Western investment and asked Soares for help in making contact. I had met Soares on a few occasions and, by chance, hosted a dinner in his honor at Hudson Pines in March. Soares told me of Machel's request and asked if I would be willing to travel to Maputo to meet him. I readily agreed.

A month later in April of 1984, accompanied by my daughter Peggy (it was her first trip to Sub-Saharan Africa) and a few colleagues, I landed in Maputo. We spent the day with Machel and then had dinner at his home with his wife Graca (who, after Machel's untimely death, would later marry Nelson Mandela) and his children. He took me into his confidence, telling me of his mistrust of the Soviets and the Cubans and his fear that Mozambique would collapse unless he received help from the West. I agreed to do what I could.

When I returned to the United States, I immediately informed Chester Crocker, the Assistant Secretary of State for Africa, of Machel's desire to open the door to talks with the United States. Gradually, as Soviet power continued to recede over the rest of the decade, a broad settlement between the White South African regime and the so-called Frontline States emerged. Eventually this would lead to the end of South African support for insurgencies throughout the region, withdrawal of Cuban troops from Angola, Namibian independence, and the transformation of South Africa itself. While this meeting was only a small step along the way to the resolution of the raging wars through all of Southern Africa at the time, I think I may have played a helpful role. Unfortunately, Samora Machel did not live to see any of these changes. He was killed in an airplane crash in 1986.

As a result of this meeting, my daughter Peggy and Graca Machel began a strong friendship that endures to this day.

Enjoying a pleasant moment with Mandela in Capetown, South Africa, September 9, 1995.

NELSON MANDELA
President of South Africa • 1994-1999

People occasionally ask who is the most inspiring person I have met during my lifetime. I always think first of Nelson Mandela - a man I treasure as a close friend.

Mandela spent twenty-seven years in South African jails, more than twenty of them in the Robben Island maximum-security prison, a barren, wind-swept rock a few miles off the coast of Capetown. Afrikaners, the small, white minority of Dutch origin who ruled South Africa with an iron hand for more than fifty years, considered Mandela a threat to "the security of their country" and convicted him of terrorism. In fact, his real "crime" was implacable opposition to apartheid, the rigid system of racial segregation that controlled the lives of all South Africans and consigned every non-white to a life of misery, degradation and poverty. Mandela struggled against that system as a young lawyer and eventually took up arms against it with his comrades in the African National Congress. Their willingness to use violence to oppose a system completely resistant to change and to sacrifice their lives, rather than to yield to injustice and oppression, resulted in years of torment for many and death for some.

I visited Robben Island and saw Mandela's cell - barely four feet by eight. When he wasn't there he was crouched in the prison yard with a hammer breaking rocks into gravel ten hours a day.

Mandela emerged from prison in 1990 a deeply embittered man, but also a hero to most of the world. He remained committed to the overthrow of apartheid and suddenly found that goal within his reach. But, he realized that if he were to lead all South Africans into the future and not preside over a blood bath to avenge decades of official terror and oppression, he would have to put aside personal hatred.

Mandela's dedication to reconciliation helped lead his nation into a new age of multi-racial democracy. His countrymen elected him President of South Africa on April 27, 1994. To the surprise of many, but not me, the country has held together over the intervening years.

I did not meet Mandela until 1993. I found him a man of enormous personal integrity and charm. During his first visit to the United States, he stayed for several days at Kykuit and greatly enjoyed the serenity of the Rockefeller Estate.

I have always lived in - and loved - New York City. Over the years, I have tried to spearhead efforts to unite the City's private sector with government so that business and political leaders could work together to better serve the public. In 1979, I cofounded and became the first chairman of the New York City Partnership, dedicated to economic development and effective governance in New York City through private-public partnerships. I am proud that today, 30 years later, the Partnership remains an influential voice in the City. In my efforts as a "citizen" of New York, I have known most of the municipal leaders who have passed through the City's portals. Following are recollections about some of the more memorable City leaders I have met.

New York City Leaders

Fiorello H. LaGuardia

Robert Moses

John V. Lindsay

Abraham Beame

Edward I. Koch

Rudolph W. Giuliani

Michael R. Bloomberg

Brooke Astor

The "Little Flower" giving me my marching orders sometime in 1940 when I served as his secretary.

FIORELLO H. LAGUARDIA
Mayor of New York City • 1933-1945

A three-term Republican mayor of New York (1934-45), known as the "Little Flower," LaGuardia was tough-minded and politically astute. He led the City through the worst years of the Great Depression by modernizing government so that it could deliver a broader range of public services. LaGuardia's strong relationship with President Franklin Roosevelt and the Democratic Party ensured a steady stream of federal dollars to pay for the City's physical infrastructure of bridges, highways, sewer systems, schools and public housing - cementing his standing with organized labor. LaGuardia was immensely popular with almost everyone in the city, including me.

I was fortunate enough to work for him for a year in 1941, just after I had finished my dissertation. LaGuardia was demanding, profane and temperamental. As his secretary, I worked closely with him on everything that crossed his desk. Sometimes that "desk" was his huge seven-passenger Chrysler limousine, equipped with flashing lights, siren and a police radio within which we sped around town to meetings, rallies and other events. I remember attending the opening of a new Sanitation Department facility in Brooklyn, built with money provided by the Federal government. The audience was the student body of a local grade school. He waved to the children and immediately launched into a paean of praise for the Works Progress Administration for providing jobs during the Depression and the Sanitation Department for its role in protecting public health. From there he moved smoothly into a celebration of democracy and the United States as an exemplar of freedom. The children were spellbound and the sanitation workers felt like heroes. By the end of the speech, I had tears in my eyes! It had been impromptu, but it came from LaGuardia's heart and it was enormously effective.

My year with LaGuardia demonstrated to me that government, properly managed and its resources thoughtfully deployed, could contribute to social progress. I learned a lot from the mayor and tried to follow his example in my own career.

With the "Power Broker" towards the end of his career, March, 1964.

ROBERT MOSES

New York City Parks Commissioner • 1934-1960
Head, Triborough Bridge and New York City Tunnel Authority • 1946-1968

My first experience with the legendary city planner and builder was when I worked for Mayor LaGuardia. While LaGuardia's other commissioners would shudder when the "Little Flower" erupted - Bob Moses would give as good as he got. He would occasionally storm right into the Mayor's office, and the two of them would argue so loudly, they could be heard all around City Hall.

Moses was a difficult man, possibly even ruthless, and he demanded total control of projects. After World War II, I always approached him carefully with ideas I thought would interest him, because his approval was needed to move forward. I had an advantage here because his chief of staff, Robert Lebwohl, was a close friend of my associate, Warren T. (Lindy) Lindquist. Lindy would often lay the groundwork with Lebwohl, who would then test the waters with his boss. Once Lindy received tentative approval, I would approach Moses with the broader proposal.

This model usually worked, as it did in the mid 1950s with the idea to build a new Chase headquarters in Lower Manhattan. When the idea of building on two contiguous downtown blocks was proposed - a revolutionary idea at the time - we needed City Planning Commission Chairman Moses' permission to permanently close part of a city street. Jack McCloy sent me to visit Moses to broach the idea and, to my great relief, he couldn't have been more accommodative. Moses understood immediately that this dramatic new building might be the catalyst Wall Street needed. At the same time, he urged me to organize business leaders to lobby on behalf of downtown's redevelopment. This was the impetus for creating the Downtown-Lower Manhattan Association, which along with the construction of One Chase Manhattan Plaza did lead to the spectacular renaissance of Lower Manhattan.

The relationship I enjoyed with the fabled power broker was unusual. While others lived in fear of the famous Moses temper - and my brother Nelson considered him an implacable adversary who had to be removed from power - our association was always civil and based on mutual respect. Perhaps Moses saw in me a kindred spirit, as eager as he was to expand the city's landscape and infrastructure. While Moses' methods may frequently have been brusque and off-putting, few can question his legacy of highways, bridges, parks and many other innovative projects. As Robert Caro, a Moses biographer, noted, New York would not necessarily have been a better city without Bob Moses, but it certainly would have been a different city.

A young Congressman Lindsay lunches with my colleagues and me at the Chase Bank, July, 1963.

John V. Lindsay
Mayor of New York City • 1966-1973

November 1958 saw the election of Nelson as governor of New York State, a moment of great achievement for him and vindication for the Rockefeller family. We all gathered at Kykuit that year to celebrate Christmas, and we took the opportunity to hold a Brothers Meeting. Nelson's triumph held our attention that day, but, after he finished outlining his plans for the future, I spoke about John Lindsay's election to Congress as the representative from the Upper East Side of New York, where most of us lived. I recounted how impressed I was with Lindsay's youthful energy, thoughtful approach to problems and enormous popular appeal. I said I thought Lindsay had a real future in politics and that we Brothers should be supportive of him. When I finished I noticed Nelson's eyes had a steely glint that meant he was not pleased with what he had just heard.

And, he wasn't. Nelson viewed Lindsay - tall, handsome, Yale-educated, and well spoken - as a rival and not someone to support. But, as Nelson's political fortunes waned over the following years, as a result of his divorce and remarriage and the conservative insurgency within the Republican Party, Lindsay's star rose. He left Congress in 1965 to run for mayor; when he won in a landslide, I believed he was headed for greatness.

Sadly for Lindsay, almost as quickly as his star ascended, it began to descend. The day after he took office, the city's transit unions went out on strike, crippling the City for almost two weeks. To make matters worse, Lindsay caved in to the excessive salary demands of union boss, Mike Quill. That set the pattern for the balance of his terms in office. Elected on a platform that promised good management, low taxes and a balanced budget, Lindsay faced a series of strikes from other municipal workers, the most serious of which shut down the City school system for almost six months. In the end, Lindsay bowed to their demands as well and in the process lost complete control of the budget. As a result of his weakness, the City suffered and John Lindsay's fortunes faded.

In the end, many years after his political career had flamed out, John Lindsay died alone in a New York City apartment.

Mayor Beame struggling through his final days as Mayor, August 4, 1977. Louise Nevelson is also pictured.

Abraham Beame
Mayor of New York City • 1974-1977

With the possible exception of Peter Stuyvesant, Abe Beame was the unluckiest mayor in New York City's history. Beame took office on January 1, 1974, succeeding the charismatic John Lindsay, and that may have been the high point of the diminutive mayor's four-year term. Disaster soon followed.

For more than a decade, the City responded to the multiple crises of the period - rising crime, racial unrest, deteriorating infrastructure, failing schools - by throwing more and more money at the problems in a feverish attempt to find solutions. Between 1965 and 1975, the City's operating budget more than tripled. Welfare rolls and public employment soared, with the increasingly powerful municipal unions pushing up the cost of wages and benefits to ever-higher levels. Local property and income taxes paid for all of this, and by the early 1970s these levies reached unsustainable levels, which drove businesses large and small from the city and weakened the local economy even further. As a result, City officials turned to an array of questionable financial practices – some of them barely legal - to balance the budget.

Ultimately they failed. The system collapsed in 1975, when it became impossible for the major commercial banks, the Chase among them, to market municipal bonds. Without that source of revenue, the City could not pay its bills or cover the salaries of hundreds of thousands of its employees. The City teetered on the edge of bankruptcy, and the banks assumed center stage.

Initially, the mayor responded to the crisis by scapegoating the banks. He accused Chase and the other major financial institutions of "disloyalty to the city" by failing to market the securities! That demagogic canard actually seemed plausible to many people. I realized that the public had to be informed of the real cause of the crisis and how it might be solved. At a summit meeting in January of 1975, Walter Wriston of Citibank, Pat Patterson of Morgan and I told the ashen-faced mayor and his panic stricken subalterns that they had to do everything in their power to bring revenue in line with expenditures in order for the markets to respond. We repeated that to the press.

The mayor refused, at first, but eventually acquiesced and followed our advice. It took years for the City to work its way out of the mess it had created. I can't recall another time when the banks played a more direct role in managing New York's financial and legal affairs. For a period of about six weeks, we practically lived at City Hall and Gracie Mansion - and on the front pages of the tabloids.

Walt, Pat and I met with Mayor Beame almost daily for a few months during the most intense period of the Fiscal Crisis. Throughout that time, I felt that Mayor Beame never understood the true nature of the problem - the City had been living beyond its means for years. Undoubtedly, Abe Beame was a good man who had the best of intentions. But, he was woefully inadequate to the task he faced as mayor of the world's greatest city.

I joined the exuberant and irrepressible Ed Koch for the groundbreaking ceremony at Windsor Terrace, a project initiated by the New York City Partnership, December 8, 1983. Also pictured, Frank Macchiarola, Senator Al D'Amato, and Lt. Gov. Mario Cuomo, standing to my left.

EDWARD I. KOCH
Mayor of New York City • 1978-1989

Ed Koch became mayor as the City was still struggling through the painful aftermath of the disastrous Fiscal Crisis. Born on the Lower East Side of New York, Koch was a quintessential New Yorker - intelligent and energetic, but blunt-spoken and thin-skinned. He thought that if you had a slightly different view of an issue that made you an enemy who had to be destroyed. He and I had a number of notable confrontations over the years, but in the end figured out ways to work together effectively. Koch learned his politics in the brutal, internecine warfare of the Democratic Clubs. Elected to Congress from the so-called "Silk Stocking" District in 1968, he earned a reputation as an extremely liberal Democrat. During his career, Koch never saw a spending program he wouldn't vote for and displayed a deep antipathy towards big business, which was surprising when you considered what most of his constituents, including me, did for a living.

Soon after Koch became mayor, I became the chairman of the New York City Partnership, a new organization dedicated to bringing the resources, talent and energy of the private sector to bear on solving the city's problems. We developed plans to deal with unemployment, the high crime rate, reforming the school system, affordable housing and economic development, including a new convention center and Westway. Koch intially dismissed the Partnership as just another special interest group and refused to meet with us. However, when we convinced our member corporations to hire more than 100,000 unemployed minority youth in the summer of 1980, Koch realized we could be allies rather than enemies and the relationship between Wall Street and City Hall improved tremendously.

Koch understood that the Fiscal Crisis had destroyed the old New York politics - characterized by high taxes, an impenetrable regulatory system, antipathy towards private business, and a particularly pernicious form of interest group politics. To his credit, Koch helped bring a new and more effective system of public management into being.

I joined Rudy Giuliani and my nephew, Rodman Rockefeller, at the dedication of the Nelson A. Rockefeller Park in Battery Park City, June 12, 1996.

RUDOLPH W. GIULIANI
Mayor of New York City • 1994-2001

Rudy Giuliani was a fiery mayor, who helped restore the city's prominence, after the uninspiring - some would argue, "disastrous" - mayoral term of David Dinkins.

Rudy's two terms were marked by improvements in the quality of New York City life and a sharp reduction in crime. That was the good part. Less good was his divisiveness. He governed in an authoritarian manner and believed if you were not with him you were against him.

For example, when Bob Kiley, the president of the New York City Partnership, criticized the Giuliani budget, the mayor effectively shut out the Partnership from participating in his Administration. Instead, he organized a Mayor's Advisory Committee of others and me, which was essentially a window dressing group that had breakfast with the mayor at Gracie Mansion every two months.

On the other hand, the one time I asked Mayor Giuliani for something, he came up big. In 1996, wearing my MoMA hat, I went to see him along with Ron Lauder (whom Rudy had bested in an acrimonious primary election three years earlier). Ron and I were there to seek $65 million in City aid for the Museum of Modern Art's expansion. We were prepared with a detailed study that showed how much MoMA contributed to the City. After we had made our case, Giuliani looked at me and said, "David, you've given so much to the City over the years, and you've never asked for anything. This is an unusual request, but I intend to grant it."

Rudy Giuliani's finest moment came in the aftermath of the destruction of the Twin Towers in the September 11, 2001 terrorist attack. His courage and compassion calmed the City and reassured the country that someone was in charge. While his tireless work in the months following the event was not enough to win the Republican nomination for president in 2008, Giuliani will forever be remembered for his leadership during that terrible time.

Mike Bloomberg and I at the 50th Anniversary of the Downtown-Lower Manhattan Association, March 18, 2008.

MICHAEL R. BLOOMBERG

Current Mayor of New York City

Mike Bloomberg began his Wall Street career in the late 1960s with Salomon Brothers. He rose steadily through the ranks, managing the firm's equity trading, sales and systems development. Mike realized that Wall Street's lifeblood was accurate and timely information, and that there was precious little of it available. He also understood that the computer revolution had made the instantaneous supply of this information possible for the first time. He left Salomon Brothers in 1981 to form Bloomberg L. P., a software company that sold terminals carrying all matter of financial information updated on a continuous basis. Before long, every desk in every brokerage house and bank around the world had his signature black monitor and green screen transmitting information to a data-hungry world. Bloomberg's innovation did not create twenty-four hour financial markets, but it certainly made them more efficient and provided an essential element in the communications infrastructure needed for global financial integration.

Bloomberg followed this tour de force with an equally impressive accomplishment - a successful tenure as mayor of the world's most important city. Few businessmen had been able to make this kind of transition, but Bloomberg's pragmatic management skills served him well as mayor. He appointed excellent people to City Hall jobs, gave them autonomy in decision-making and practiced a results-based approach to municipal governance. It worked. The City's economy expanded, school reform was implemented and a watchful eye was kept on the budget. He found ways to persuade the city's many different ethnic groups to work together, and his administration has been remarkably free of scandal.

The mayor has been a generous philanthropist, often using his own substantial financial resources to support projects critical to the City's future. His PLANYC is a visionary effort to make New York more energy efficient and environmentally sound to adjust the metropolis to the radically new circumstances of the 21st century, while maintaining its status as the world's financial capital. The plan includes planting a million new trees throughout all five boroughs to help absorb greenhouses gases. The City will pay for most of the cost, but private funds were also needed. I offered to match the mayor's $5 million personal contribution to ensure that trees would also be planted around city-owned housing projects and public schools. The mayor and I announced the program at the Jefferson Houses in East Harlem on Earth Day in 2008.

The trees program is just one example of Mike Bloomberg's understanding of what the City needed and his ability to contribute officially and personally to answer the City's challenges. I'm of the mind that next to Fiorello LaGuardia, Mike Bloomberg was as good a mayor as New York has ever seen.

Peggy and I often visited Brooke at her home Holly Hill. This photograph was taken in the early 1990s.

BROOKE ASTOR
1902-2007

Brooke was one of the most remarkable women I have ever known - a gifted writer, an inspiring teacher and a thoughtful philanthropist - the "leading lady of New York" in every sense of the word.

Brooke's third husband, Vincent Astor, was a descendant of John Jacob Astor, who was the richest man in America when he died in 1848. Vincent took over management of the family business after his father's death on the Titanic in 1912 and spent the rest of his life trying to restore the family fortune. He succeeded to a remarkable degree. Brooke and Vincent married in the early 1950s. They were an oddly matched pair. Vincent was shy, almost reclusive; Brooke loved to entertain and embraced the whirl of New York Society. Shortly before his death in 1959, Vincent established a foundation and named Brooke its sole trustee.

Brooke devoted much of her time and financial resources (almost $250 million) to helping New Yorkers from every walk of life. She considered it her duty to visit all the homeless shelters, childcare centers, schools and libraries supported by the Vincent Astor Foundation. She always wore a beautiful dress and a stylish hat on these visits, as if she were calling on the Queen of England (whom she knew quite well!).

Brooke was always great fun. For her 100th birthday party, my brother Laurance and I hosted a party at the Playhouse on the Kykuit Estate. We invited 100 of Brooke's relatives and closest friends. Every table had its own cake in the form of a hat. One highlight of the evening was the dance that Brooke and I shared; her nimble feet never missed a beat.

I visited her often during her last years. She was quite frail, but always insisted that I give her two or three affectionate kisses. In the summer of 2006, I became involved in the effort to ensure that Brooke lived out her last days in comfort and dignity. I joined with others in petitioning the court to appoint a guardian to manage her affairs. We achieved our goal. Brooke returned to her beloved Holly Hill, where her closest friends, her long time staff and her dogs, Boysie and Girlsie, surrounded her. She died there on August 13, 2007 at the age of 105.

PHOTOGRAPHIC CREDITS

Photographs are listed in their order of appearance with credit given to the
organization or indivual providing the image. The photographer's name is given when known.

David Rockefeller
JPMorgan Chase Archives. Art Lavine.

David Rockefeller on Kharg Island, Iran, 1969.
JPMorgan Chase Archives.

David Rockefeller in Northern Syria, World War II, 1944.
David Rockefeller Collection.

David Rockefeller in car on the Pocantico estate in the mid 1930s.
David Rockefeller Collection.

Photo taken with Brownie camera during trip to Egypt, Spring, 1929.
David Rockefeller Collection.

Adolph Hitler leading the funeral cortege for Field Marshall Eric Ludendorff,
Munich, Germany, December, 1937.
David Rockefeller Collection.

The White House
Getty Images. Mia Klein.

Calvin Coolidge
Library of Congress/Getty Images.

Dwight Eisenhower
Time Life Pictures/Getty Images. George Silk.

John F. Kennedy
JPMorgan Chase Archives. White House photo.

Lyndon B. Johnson
JPMorgan Chase Archives. White House photo.

Richard M. Nixon
JPMorgan Chase Archives. White House photo.

Gerald R. Ford
JPMorgan Chase Archives. (1)
Kennedy/Getty Images. David Hume. (2)

Jimmy Carter
JPMorgan Chase Archives. White House photo.

Ronald Reagan
David Rockefeller Collection.

George H. W. Bush
JPMorgan Chase Archives. White House photo.

William Clinton
David Rockefeller Collection. White House photo.

George W. Bush
David Rockefeller Collection.

The Sphinx taken with Brownie camera during trip to Egypt, Spring, 1929.
David Rockefeller Collection.

Yasser Arafat
David Rockefeller Collection. Jeff Reinke.

Menachem Begin
David Rockefeller Collection.

Moshe Dayan
David Rockefeller Collection.

Abdel Azis Al Ghani
JPMorgan Chase Archives.

Saddam Hussein
Time-Life Pictures/Getty Images. Peter Jordan.

Sheik Isa bin Salman al Khalifa
JPMorgan Chase Archives.

Teddy Kollek
JPMorgan Chase Archives.

Golda Meir
JPMorgan Chase Archives.

Molay Hassan ben Mohammad
David Rockefeller Collection.

Sheik Zayed al Nahyan
JPMorgan Chase Archives.

Gamal Abdel Nasser
ASP/Getty Images. Stringer.

Mohammad Reza Pahlavi
JPMorgan Chase Archives.

Yitzhak Rabin
JPMorgan Chase Archives.

Anwar al Sadat
JPMorgan Chase Archives.

Qaboos bin Said
JPMorgan Chase Archives.

Faisal Ibn Abdul al Saud
Time Life Pictures/Getty Images. Charles Bonnay.

Ariel Sharon
AFP/Getty Images. Menahem Kahana.

Hussein bin Talal
JPMorgan Chase Archives.

David Rockefeller in Accra, Ghana, 1982.
David Rockefeller Collection.

Haile Selassie
Rockefeller Center Archives Center.

Felix Houphouet-Boigny
David Rockefeller Collection.

Sekou Touré
Both photographs, David Rockefeller Collection.

Kenneth Kaunda
JPMorgan Chase Archives. Art Lavine.

Jomo Kenyatta
Fox Photos/Getty Images. George Freston.

Omar Bongo
JPMorgan Chase Archives.

Samora Machel
Getty Images. Agence France Presse photo.

Nelson Mandela
David Rockefeller Collection.

New York City Skyline
David Rockefeller Collection.